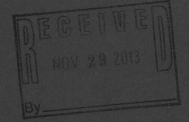

ART DETECTIVE

SPOT THE DIFFERENCE!

Doris Kutschbach
Illustrated by Julia Dürr

PRESTEL

Munich · London · New York

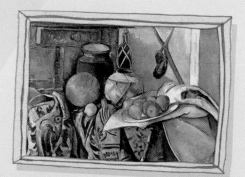

HELLO! My name is Carl, but my friends call me Charlie the Sleuth.

I'm a detective who solves art crimes, and right now I'm working on a very difficult case. It's about a shady artist and his forgeries—paintings he offers for sale that aren't really what they appear to be.

When I first saw these paintings, I knew right away something was fishy. Some of them looked almost exactly like famous artworks from museums! The artist must have copied the famous original paintings and tried to sell them as genuine. But his forgeries were truly impressive. If you didn't know the original pictures, you'd never guess that these were fakes.

This is where things start getting complicated. In order to convict the person who made the forgeries, I have to find the mistakes in his pictures, which isn't easy.

Do you think you could help? If you compare the forgeries very carefully to the original works, I'm sure you'll be able to detect a few differences. Let's start by examining this picture here…

THE SUNDAY STROLL
PAINTED BY CARL SPITZWEG ...

ORIGINAL

... AND PAINTED BY AN ART FORGER

FORGERY

Can you find the differences? The forger made **15** mistakes.

A SUNDAY AFTERNOON
ON THE ISLAND OF LA GRANDE JATTE
BY GEORGES SEURAT

15 mistakes are hidden here.

ORIGINAL

FORGERY

Can you find **20** mistakes?

EXOTIC LANDSCAPE WITH MONKEYS PLAYING
BY HENRI ROUSSEAU

Can you detect **15** differences?

BY THE SEA
BY PAUL GAUGUIN

ORIGINAL

LUNCH IN THE GARDEN
BY CLAUDE MONET

ORIGINAL

Look, there's
Jean ...

FORGERY

Can you find the **15** mistakes?

STILL LIFE WITH GINGER JAR AND EGGPLANTS
BY PAUL CÉZANNE

ORIGINAL

Mmmm, scrumptious!

20 mistakes have crept in here.

FORGERY

7 mice are hiding here.
Can you figure out what they've eaten or nibbled?

original ↑

Can you find the **20** differences between the original and the fake?

BARELY IN LEAF
BY PAUL KLEE

ORIGINAL

No, I don't have any bird-seed...

FORGERY

Can you discover the forger's **20** mistakes?

And can you find the other **10** birds?

A PANEL FROM THE GRABOW ALTARPIECE PAINTED BY MASTER BERTRAM

ORIGINAL

25 mistakes have snuck in here.

THE TOWER OF BABEL
BY PIETER BRUEGHEL

ORIGINAL

This picture is really old, and they're still not finished building the tower!

FORGERY

Find **25** differences.

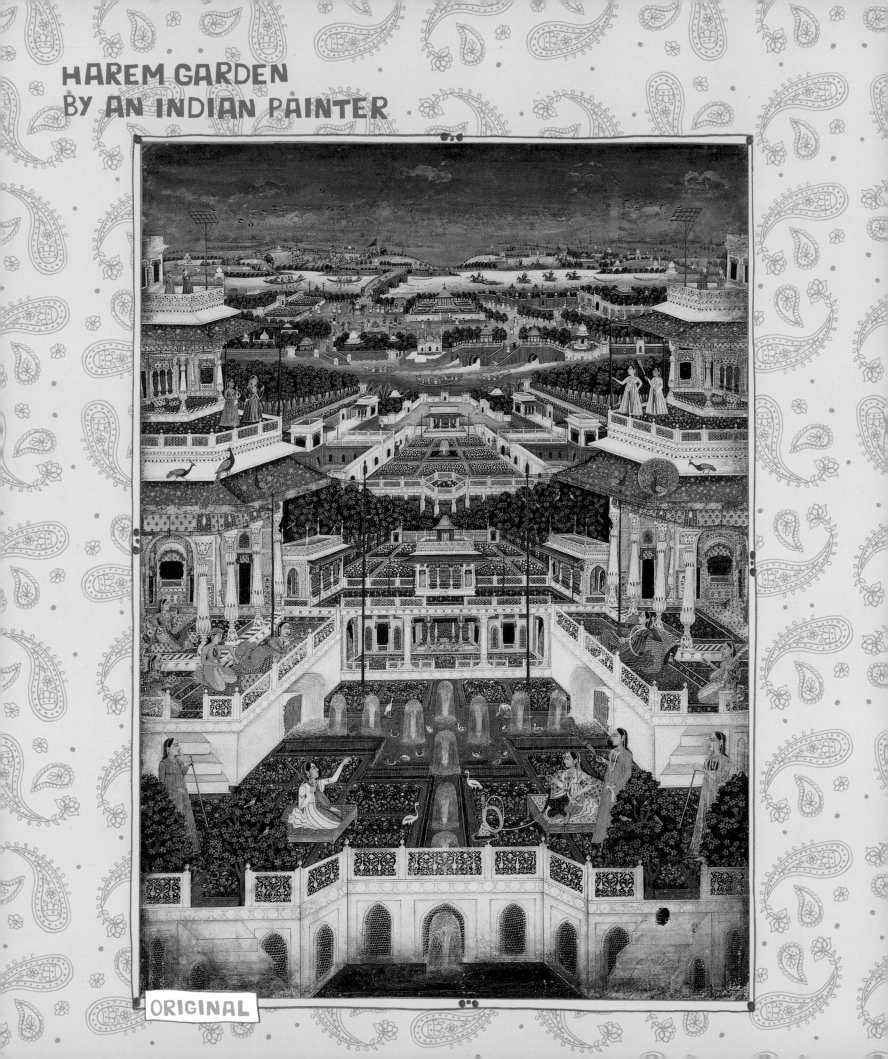

FORGERY

LOCK AT DOLO ON THE BRENTA
BY CANALETTO

Can you find the **25** mistakes?

THE AMBASSADORS
BY HANS HOLBEIN THE YOUNGER

Have a look at this strange
thing from down here – you'll
be surprised!

original

forgery

The forger made **15** mistakes. Can you find them?

PLACE DU THÉÂTRE IN PARIS
BY CAMILLE PISSARRO

ORIGINAL

FORGERY

Paris sure is a busy place...

Can you find **20** differences?

BRANDENBURG GATE
BY ERNST LUDWIG KIRCHNER

ORIGINAL

FORGERY

CARNATION, LILY, LILY, ROSE
BY JOHN SINGER SARGENT

ORIGINAL

FORGERY

How many differences can you discover here?

FORGERY

13...14...15...

I've found all the mistakes!

SOLUTIONS

Excellent, I think we've done it. We have enough evidence to convict the art forger. Here you can double check if you were able to spot all the differences. And if you're interested, there's also information about each of the original works in the museums.

THE SUNDAY STROLL, 1841
CARL SPITZWEG (1808-1885)

Carl Spitzweg lived in Munich, Germany, and he liked to paint small scenes taken from the daily lives of people around him. This picture is even a little funny. The small procession is led by the portly papa with his Sunday hat held aloft on his walking stick. The little child holding his hand is barely visible above the high grass. The rest of the family follows in single file in long dresses and large hats. Most people today would rather wear jeans and a t-shirt in their spare time. But families back then donned their finest clothes on Sunday, even for a walk in the meadow.

Museum Carolino-Augusteum, Salzburg, Austria · Photo: Blauel/Gnamm – Artothek

A SUNDAY AFTERNOON ON THE ISLAND OF LA GRANDE JATTE, 1884-1886
GEORGES SEURAT (1859-1891)

The people in this summer picture are also dressed in their Sunday best. The painting shows a Sunday afternoon on the island of La Grande Jatte, which lies near Paris in the River Seine. French artist Georges Seurat, who made this artwork, invented a new painting technique. He composed his pictures with many small dabs of color. From up close, the pictures look like masses of small dots. Only when you move farther back does your eye blend the colors together. This technique makes Seurat's pictures look especially bright and luminous.

The Art Institute of Chicago, USA · Photo: Joseph S. Martin – Artothek

THE MONEYCHANGER AND HIS WIFE, 1514
QUINTEN MASSYS (1465/66-1531)

The painter of this picture lived in the Netherlands. Many wealthy merchants lived there as well, and they could afford expensive works of art. Here we see a "moneychanger," an early type of banker, and his wife. Clearly, this couple has a lot of money! And look at how meticulously the painter rendered every detail. Many of the objects in the picture had specific meanings—such as the scales, which were considered a symbol of justice.

Musée du Louvre, Paris, France

EXOTIC LANDSCAPE WITH MONKEYS PLAYING, 1910
HENRI ROUSSEAU (1844–1910)

Henri Rousseau lived in Paris and had nine children with his wife. He worked as a toll collector, which is why he is also known as "the customs officer." Rousseau was friends with many poets and painters. But he longed to be an artist himself, and he painted whenever he had spare time. Many of his paintings depict the jungle, where he had never actually been. Rousseau learned about tropical plants by visiting the greenhouse at Paris's botanical garden.

Norton Simon Collection, Pasadena, USA · Photo: Peter Willi – Artothek

BY THE SEA, 1892
PAUL GAUGUIN (1848–1903)

The painter Paul Gauguin was one of Rousseau's friends, and he too dreamed of far-away lands. One day he left his family, boarded a ship, and sailed for the distant island of Tahiti. Gauguin spent much of the rest of his life in the South Seas. He became famous for his brilliantly-colored images of the plants and beautiful people in this exotic region.

National Gallery, Washington, USA

LUNCH IN THE GARDEN, c. 1873
CLAUDE MONET (1840–1926)

The little boy playing in the garden was Jean, the eldest son of painter Claude Monet. He was around six years old when his father painted this picture. At the time the Monet family lived in Argenteuil, near Paris. They were bitterly poor, since no one wanted to buy Monet's paintings … yet. Here the painter has not portrayed his poverty, however, but the warm rays of the sun and the delightful colors of the flower garden. This kind of art, called Impressionism, would become fashionable a few years later—and Monet and his family would become wealthy.

Musée du Louvre, Paris, France · Photo: Peter Willi – Artothek

STILL LIFE WITH GINGER JAR AND EGGPLANTS, 1893/94
PAUL CÉZANNE (1839–1906)

Paul Cézanne was a lone wolf. He lived a secluded life in southern France—his house there in Aix-en-Provence can still be visited today. Over and over again he painted fruits and vegetables, like the apples and pears from his garden. He also depicted objects that stood around his studio, including the round-bellied ginger jar. Cézanne never got bored of these things: in each picture he arranged them differently on the thick, patterned tablecloths.

The Metropolitan Museum, New York, USA · Photo: Artothek

STILL LIFE WITH PARROT, EARLY 1600s
GEORG FLEGEL (1566-1638)

No one knows exactly when Georg Flegel painted this picture. At the time —it was a period in art history called the Baroque—still lifes were very popular. These pictures depict food, flowers, musical instruments, or other objects, often in careful arrangements. Rich people during Flegel's time liked the still life because it showed off their wealth. But this kind of picture often had hidden messages as well. For example, it could remind the viewer that everything in life is impermanent: fruit rots, flowers wilt, and even human life ends.

Alte Pinakothek, Munich, Germany

BIRDS, 1914
FRANZ MARC (1880-1916)

Franz Marc's birds look very different from Georg Flegel's parrot. The whole picture is filled with excited fluttering, the forms are as sharp as splinters, and the colors are intensely bright. Marc mostly painted animals, but it was not so important for him to paint them as they actually looked. Instead, he wanted to paint the world from the animals' point of view and use intense colors to express his own feelings.

Städtische Galerie im Lenbachhaus, Munich, Germany · Photo: Hans Hinz – Artothek

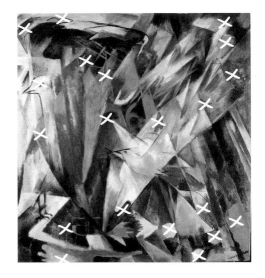

BARELY IN LEAF, 1934
PAUL KLEE (1879-1940)

Paul Klee loved poetry, art, and music, and for a long time he wasn't able to decide which of these he loved best. In the end he became a very poetic painter, whose pictures seem filled with delicate musical tones. This picture—with its branches, leaves, and berries—sounds like a soft autumn song. Klee painted the work while living in Switzerland. He and his family had just fled from Germany and its Nazi government, which didn't like modern artists.

Galerie Beyeler, Basel, Switzerland · Photo: Hans Hinz – Artothek

A PANEL FROM THE GRABOW ALTARPIECE, c. 1380
MASTER BERTRAM (ACTIVE ARROUND 1340-1414/15)

The German painter Master Bertram painted many scenes from the Bible on this wooden panel. In the upper row God can be seen creating the plants, the animals, and the first man, Adam. Beneath this picture are other stories from the Old Testament (the sacrifice of Isaac, Isaac refusing Esau his blessing, and Isaac blessing Jacob). The panel belongs to an enormous painting called an altarpiece, which had many more images. This artwork originally stood in the Church of St. Peter in Hamburg, Germany. Today it can be seen in Hamburg's Kunsthalle museum, where a small model allows you to open and close the painting's moveable "wings," or sides.

Hamburger Kunsthalle, Hamburg, Germany · Photo: The Bridgeman Art Library

THE TOWER OF BABEL, 1563
PIETER BRUEGHEL THE ELDER (1524/30–1569)

In this picture by Pieter Brueghel, you can see how buildings were constructed around 450 years ago—large cranes and bulldozers didn't yet exist. The story of the Tower of Babel comes from the Book of Genesis in the Bible, and it tells how all the world's people originally spoke the same language. One day they began to build a tower that would reach up into heaven. This made God angry, however, because heaven was not a place for living people. So God "confused" their languages, making it impossible for them to communicate with each other and finish the tower.

Kunsthistorisches Museum, Vienna, Austria · Photo: Photobusiness – Artothek

HAREM GARDEN, 1700s
UNKNOWN INDIAN PAINTER

This painting, which reveals an endless number of small details and stories, comes from India. It shows the harem—a house in which women and girls lived—of an Indian prince, or maharaja. The prince must have been very rich to have such magnificent palaces and gardens. Many Indian painters' names are unknown to us, and often several painters worked together on the same artwork.

David Collection, Copenhagen, Denmark

LOCK AT DOLO ON THE BRENTA, c. 1732/35
GIOVANNI ANTONIO CANAL, CALLED CANALETTO (1697–1768)

Italian painter Canaletto is famous for his views of Venice, which during his day were all the rage among the city's English tourists. Since photography did not yet exist, paintings with city views were highly sought-after souvenirs. The city of Dolo, which Canaletto depicted in this painting, lies on the Brenta Canal connecting the cities of Padua and Venice. The water there was dammed up, and the large lock was used to raise or lower the canal's water level so that ships could pass through.

Staatsgalerie Stuttgart, Stuttgart, Germany

THE AMBASSADORS, 1533
HANS HOLBEIN THE YOUNGER (1497/98–1543)

Hans Holbein came from Germany, but he was living in England when he painted this work. The two men depicted here were friends and must have been highly educated: the painting shows them with astronomical and mathematical devices, books, and musical instruments. If you look at the picture at an angle from the lower left, you'll be able to make out the strange object at their feet: it's a distorted image of a skull!

National Gallery, London, United Kingdom

PLACE DU THÉÂTRE IN PARIS, 1898
CAMILLE PISSARRO (1830–1903)

The French artist Camille Pissarro was a friend of Claude Monet, whom you've already met above. Like Monet, Pissarro was a member of the group of artists in Paris known as Impressionists. These artists did not want their pictures to tell great stories or portray important people. Instead, they tried capture life's fleeting moments: the light of the noontime sun, the atmosphere of a rainy day, the view of a square in Paris on a cloudy afternoon…

County Museum, Los Angeles,USA · Photo: Artothek

BRANDENBURG GATE, 1929
ERNST LUDWIG KIRCHNER (1880–1938)

Are you surprised that things in this painting have completely different colors than in reality? This painting style is called Expressionism. Expressionist artists did not want to depict the outward apperance of reality. Instead, they used intense colors and wild shapes to express their inner feelings. They wanted to show things as they themselves experienced them. Perhaps German artist Ernst Ludwig Kirchner found life in Berlin cold and forbidding. Here he painted the square in front of Berlin's Brandenburg Gate in a somber, chilly blue.

Städel Museum, Frankfurt am Main, Germany · Photo: Städel Museum – Artothek

CARNATION, LILY, LILY, ROSE, 1885/86
JOHN SINGER SARGENT (1856–1925)

As a child, the American artist John Singer Sargent travelled a great deal with his parents—so much, in fact, that he was rarely in school. Instead, he spent a lot of time in museums. Even as an adult, he never stayed long in one place. Sargent travelled all over Europe, living in Rome, Paris, Dresden, Venice, and London, among other places. The two girls in this painting are named Dolly and Polly. They had to model for Sargent for many weeks while he attempted to capture the fleeting atmosphere of twilight in his picture.

Tate Britain, London, United Kingdom

STARRY NIGHT, 1889
VINCENT VAN GOGH (1853–1890)

Vincent van Gogh was a great painter, but no one realized this during his lifetime. His life was difficult because he made little money from his art and suffered from a mental illness. At the time Vincent painted this picture, he was living in an asylum (a hospital for the mentally ill) in Saint-Rémy-de-Provence in southern France. The wild brush strokes and whirl of paint in his starry sky give a good idea of the sick painter's emotional turmoil.

The Museum of Modern Art, New York, USA